flavouring with
Spices

flavouring with
Spices

Clare Gordon-Smith

photography by

James Merrell

RYLAND
PETERS
& SMALL

LONDON NEW YORK

Art Director **Jacqui Small**

Art Editor **Penny Stock**

Design Assistant **Mark Latter**

Editor **Elsa Petersen-Schepelern**

Photography **James Merrell**

Food Stylist **Lucy McKelvie**

Stylist **Sue Skeen**

Production Consultant **Vincent Smith**

Our thanks to Christine Walsh and Ian Bartlett, and Sally Everett of Food Link (Eastern) Ltd.

First published in the Great Britain in 1996 by
Ryland Peters & Small
Kirkman House
12–14 Whitfield Street, London W1T 2RP
www.rylandpeters.com

This paperback edition first published in 2003
10 9 8 7 6 5 4 3 2 1

Printed and bound in China

ISBN 1 84172 446 7

A CIP record for this book is available from the British Library

Notes:
Metric and imperial measurements are
given. Use one set of measurements
only and not a mixture of both.

Ovens should be preheated to the
specified temperature – if using a
fan-assisted oven, adjust time and
temperature according to the
manufacturer's instructions.

Spices are the bark, seeds, roots or pods of various aromatic plants. Once, spices like ginger and tamarind were always dried but, thanks to modern transport, some can now be found fresh.

Spice mixtures are used in all the world's great cuisines, and many use blends peculiar to their own areas, and to particular dishes. Best freshly ground, they can also be bought ready-prepared. Shown here before grinding are some of the most famous blends. Back row, from left: India's classic spice mixture, **garam masala** (recipe page 36), including cloves, pepper, cumin, cinnamon, nutmeg and mace, varies from area to area; Morocco's **ras-el-hanout**, a mix of spices, rosebuds and lavender; and the Jamaican **jerk seasoning**, moistened with garlic and lime juice, used to spice meat dishes. Front row, from left are the ingredients for **curry powder** (recipe page 16); classic **pickling spice** with mustard seeds, peppercorns, mace, chillies, allspice and dill seed; and traditional European **mixed spice**, with nutmeg, cinnamon, ginger and cloves, used in Christmas puddings and cakes.

the flavours of
Spices

Cassia bark

Paprika

Nutmeg

Mace

Vanilla pods

Caraway seeds

Mustard seeds

Ginger

Saffron

Star anise

A selection of spices – fresh, dried, flaked or ground. **Cassia bark** is sometimes used instead of cinnamon. Powdered **paprika** from Hungary ranges in taste from mild to hot. Black **mustard seeds** are used in India and Nepal, as well as in prepared mustards. Whole **nutmegs** are best freshly grated, but ground nutmeg is widely available. Russet-coloured **mace**, the lacy covering of the nutmeg, can be bought whole or ground, and is more subtle than nutmeg. **Ginger,** like **horseradish** and **galangal,** is a hot, pungent root, available fresh, dried and flaked (as here). **Vanilla** pods can be used again and again, and kept in a jar of sugar (which may then be used to flavour puddings).

8 The flavours of spices

Cinnamon sticks

Turmeric powder

Turmeric roots

Tamarind pods

Black cardamom pods

Green cardamom pods

Juniper berries

Cloves

Allspice

White peppercorns

Caraway seeds flavour bread and cakes in Northern Europe. Star-shaped **star anise** has an aniseed taste. Expensive **saffron** strands are the dried stigmata of the saffron crocus. **Cinnamon** sticks are also available in ground form. Yellow **turmeric** is made from a ginger-like root. Nail-shaped **cloves** are one of the world's most popular spices.

Jamaican **allspice** has a mixed-spice flavour. Velvety fat **tamarind** pods contain lemony pulp and seeds. White peppercorns are black **pepper** with the outer shell removed. Large black and the smaller green **cardamom** pods contain lots of tiny, aromatic black seeds. Large, black **juniper** berries are the major flavouring of gin.

The flavours of spices **9**

Starters

Sautéed prawns
with turmeric and mustard seeds

India is the home of many of the world's most wonderful spices, so Indian cooks are past masters at using them in all kinds of cooking. Seaside holiday resorts in India, such as Goa and Kerala, are great places to sample spanking-fresh seafood spiced in the most interesting, unusual ways.

Peel the prawns, but leave the tail fins intact. Place the prawns in a bowl. Mix the turmeric and chilli powder together, sprinkle over the prawns, toss well and lightly rub the mixture into the flesh. Heat the oil in a large frying pan and, when very hot, add the mustard seeds. When they start popping, add the crushed garlic and fry until golden, then stir in the chopped green chilli.
Add the prawns and sauté over a high heat for about 2–3 minutes until they become opaque. Remove immediately to a serving plate – do not overcook. Sprinkle with salt and the chopped fresh coriander leaves, then serve with crispy poppadoms.

12 medium-sized
uncooked prawns

pinch of turmeric

pinch of chilli powder

4 tablespoons
sunflower oil

½ teaspoon black
mustard seeds

4 garlic cloves, crushed

1 fresh hot green chilli,
finely chopped

1 tablespoon chopped
fresh coriander leaves

coarse sea salt

crispy poppadoms,
to serve

Serves 4

Hot tortillas
stuffed with spiced crab

Crab forms a great partnership with ginger or chillies in many cuisines, all around the world. This one is based on a Mexican original, teamed with a zippy avocado salsa.

To prepare the salsa, place the avocado in a bowl and toss in the lemon juice. Stir in the remaining ingredients and set aside to develop the flavours. To prepare the filling, heat the olive oil in a non-stick pan, add the onion, garlic and ginger and cook for 2–3 minutes, until golden. Stir in the coriander, cumin, crabmeat, tomatoes, salt and pepper. Heat the tortillas in a dry frying pan, then place the filling over half of each one. Wrap the other half over the top of the filling and serve with the avocado and coriander salsa.

1 tablespoon olive oil

1 onion, finely chopped

2 garlic cloves, crushed

2.5 cm/1 inch piece of fresh ginger, crushed

1 teaspoon coriander seeds or powder

½ teaspoon cumin

250 g/8 oz fresh crabmeat

2 plum tomatoes, skinned, deseeded and chopped

salt and pepper

1 packet of tortillas

avocado salsa

1 avocado, sliced

2 teaspoons lemon juice

1 red onion, sliced

2 tablespoons chopped fresh coriander leaves

juice and grated zest of 1 lime

pinch of cayenne

salt

Serves 4

coriander and cumin are great

with crab – in an extra **spicy partnership**

Caribbean chicken
with ginger and star anise

Use chicken or vegetable stock for this recipe, and use white wine vinegar for a mild taste. You can also add sprigs of basil or rosemary for a more herby flavour.

Crush the ginger and star anise and place in a pan with the chicken, sherry and stock. Simmer for 20 minutes until the chicken is tender. Shred the chicken into thin strips and place in a bowl with the garlic, bay leaves, olive oil, vinegar, onions, salt and pepper. Mix well and leave to marinate in the refrigerator for a couple of days. Serve with spinach salad and lemon wedges

25 g/1 oz fresh ginger

3 star anise

4 chicken breasts

3 tablespoons sherry

150 ml/¼ pint stock

3 garlic cloves, crushed

2 bay leaves

150 ml/¼ pint olive oil

150 ml/¼ pint vinegar

2 white onions, sliced

salt and 8 peppercorns

Serves 4

Aubergine dip
with coriander and sesame seeds

Brush the aubergines with chilli oil and cook in a preheated oven at 200°C (400°F) Gas Mark 6 for 40 minutes until soft. Scrape the flesh into a bowl. Crush the coriander seeds, then dry-fry with the sesame seeds for 1 minute to release the flavours. Crush the garlic and ginger. Gently melt the creamed coconut in a saucepan. Mix all the ingredients together to form a paste. Place in a serving bowl and serve either warm or chilled. Pitta breads would be suitable accompaniments.

4 aubergines, halved

2 tablespoons chilli oil

25 g/1 oz coriander seeds

25 g/1 oz sesame seeds

4–6 garlic cloves

25 g/1 oz fresh ginger

25 g/1 oz creamed coconut

salt

Serves 4

Curried parsnip soup
with crème fraîche

A very British recipe – using curry powder,
that thoroughly English form of spice.
Though the British brought it back from
India, it is a spice mixture that no Indian
cook would recognize. It goes particularly
well with sweet young parsnips. Home-made
curry powder is vastly superior to the shop-
bought kind. Mix 3 tablespoons coriander
seeds with 2 tablespoons each of cumin
seeds, mustard seeds and turmeric,
1 teaspoon each of fenugreek, ground
ginger and peppercorns, plus a cinnamon
stick and 3 dried chillies. Grind in a spice or
coffee grinder, keep in an airtight jar and
use as quickly as possible.

Melt the butter in a heavy-based saucepan, stir
in the curry powder and cook for 1 minute.
Add the parsnips, salt, pepper and vegetable
stock, bring to the boil and simmer for about
20 minutes. Pour into a blender or food
processor and purée until smooth. Add extra
stock if you prefer a thinner soup.
Reheat and serve with a dollop of crème
fraîche and crusty wholegrain bread.

25 g/1 oz butter

1 tablespoon
curry powder,
preferably
home-made
(see introduction)

500 g/1 lb
young parsnips,
roughly chopped

600 ml/1 pint
vegetable stock

salt and freshly
ground black pepper

to serve

150 ml/¼ pint
crème fraîche

paprika or
curry powder,
to sprinkle

Serves 4

a classic soup **partnership** – parsnips

with curry powder to give extra zip

Jamaican pumpkin soup
with spiced cream

Cooks in Jamaica and the other Caribbean islands really know their spices! This recipe uses chillies and ground ginger in the soup and lots of spices in the cream garnish. Use chopped jalapeños for extra heat or, for an unusual, spicy, fruity flavour, a whole Scotch bonnet chilli, removed (unbroken) just before puréeing in the blender.

To make the spiced cream, place the crème fraîche in a bowl, stir in the spices, and set aside to infuse. To make the soup, peel the pumpkin, scrape out the seeds with a spoon and cut the flesh into 2.5 cm/1 inch pieces. Deseed and dice the chillies. Place the butter in a large saucepan and melt over medium heat. Add the onion, carrot and celery and sauté until softened and transparent. Stir in the garlic and chillies and cook for 1 minute. Add the pumpkin, chicken stock, herbs, ginger and seasoning. Bring to the boil, reduce the heat and simmer for 20 minutes until the vegetables are soft. Remove the bay leaves and thyme, pour into a blender or food processor, add the cream and purée until smooth. Thin with stock if necessary. Serve with a large dollop of spiced cream on top, and sprinkle with snipped chives.

500 g/1 lb pumpkin

2 jalapeño chillies

25 g/1 oz butter

1 onion, diced

1 carrot, diced

1 celery stalk, diced

3 garlic cloves, crushed

1.2 litres/2 pints chicken stock

2 bay leaves

2 sprigs of thyme

4 tablespoons chopped fresh flat leaf parsley

pinch of ground ginger

300 ml/½ pint cream

salt and pepper

spiced cream

150 ml/¼ pint crème fraîche

pinch of ground cumin

pinch of coriander

pinch of cayenne

1 bunch of chives

Serves 4

Main courses

Seared salmon
in spicy ginger marinade

They don't have salmon in Asia, but Asian spices marry wonderfully with this rich king of fishes – as demonstrated in this rather Pan-Pacific recipe. If you're serving this dish with large fennel bulbs, cut them in quarters, brush with oil and bake in a hot oven until tender and crispy brown around the edges.

To make the marinade, mix all the ingredients in a shallow bowl. Add the salmon fillet and turn to coat with the marinade. Chill for at least 2 hours. When ready to cook, remove the fish from the marinade and pat dry with kitchen paper. Dust the fish with the ground star anise. Heat a cast-iron grill pan, add the fish and sear on both sides, then serve. Roasted fennel would be a suitable accompaniment.

1 large salmon fillet, about 500 g/1 lb

pinch of ground star anise

spicy ginger marinade

2 tablespoons soy sauce

6 star anise, crushed

4 tablespoons vermouth

2.5 cm/1 inch piece of ginger, finely sliced

1 garlic clove, crushed

2 tablespoons chopped fresh coriander

1 red chilli, deseeded and chopped

Serves 4

Steamed monkfish
with creamy coconut rice

Thai cooking is one of the most interesting spice-based cuisines. This recipe uses a mixture of spices spread over the fish before steaming, and a complementary mixture to perfume the delicious, sticky Thai spiced rice, served in pretty banana leaf parcels. If you can't find banana leaves, substitute foil, or omit the final steaming of the rice.

To make the spiced rice, heat the oil in a pan, add the onion and fry gently until golden. Crush the seeds from the cardamom pods, add the seeds and seasoning to the pan, and fry for 1 minute more. Stir in the rice and creamed coconut, followed by the water and cook for about 10 minutes until tender. Drain and wrap in banana leaves.
To prepare the fish, mix all the ingredients for the spice mixture together, and press the mixture on top of the fish fillets, then place in a bamboo steamer with the banana leaf parcels, and set over a pan of simmering water. Steam for about 5 minutes until the fish becomes opaque, then serve immediately with the sliced kaffir limes.

cardamom, cumin and turmeric –

delicious with fish and creamy spiced rice

4 monkfish fillets

sliced kaffir limes

spice mixture

2.5 cm/1 inch piece of fresh ginger, grated

pinch of ground coriander

pinch of ground cumin

pinch of turmeric

2 cloves

1 onion, finely chopped

2 green chillies

1 garlic clove, crushed

coconut rice

2 tablespoons corn oil

1 small onion, diced

3 cardamom pods

375 g/12 oz Thai rice

125 g/4 oz creamed coconut, chopped

450 ml/¾ pint water

banana leaves

salt and pepper

Serves 4

Roasted cod
with a spicy, crunchy crust

Horseradish is a spice that's usually eaten fresh since, once heated, it loses much of its pungency. That isn't always a disadvantage though, as this unusual recipe proves.

To make the tartare sauce, mix all the ingredients together and set aside to develop the flavours.

To make the spicy crust, mix together the lemon rind, breadcrumbs, crushed coriander seeds, parsley, horseradish, salt and pepper.

Place the cod steaks in a shallow roasting tin and season with salt and pepper.

Press the crust mixture firmly on to the steaks. Bake in a preheated oven at 200°C (400°F) Gas Mark 6 for 10–15 minutes until the flesh is white and milky.

To serve, place the roasted cod on 4 heated dinner plates and serve the tartare sauce separately. Saffron mashed potatoes and steamed baby leeks would be suitable accompaniments.

hip-hot **horseradish** paired with crunc

an East-meets-We

araway seeds –

pice combination

4 cod steaks

salt and pepper

spicy crust

grated rind of 1 lemon

50 g/2 oz breadcrumbs

1 tablespoon crushed
coriander seeds

2 tablespoons chopped
fresh flat leaf parsley

50 g/ 2 oz freshly
grated horseradish

salt and freshly
ground black pepper

tartare sauce

6 medium gherkins,
finely chopped

250 ml/8 fl oz
crème fraîche

2 tablespoons chopped
fresh flat leaf parsley

1 teaspoon
caraway seeds

1 teaspoon
fennel seeds

salt and freshly
ground black pepper

Serves 4

Sesame roasted tuna
in orange anise marinade

Honey, oil and soy sauce make wonderful marinades. The honey helps all the flavours stick to the food, and you can vary the kind of soy sauce – dark soy has more flavour, but darkens the food; light soy is more subtle.

Place the tuna fillet in a shallow dish, whisk the marinade ingredients together, pour over the fish, and set aside for a few hours.

Place the sweet potato chips in a roasting tin, sprinkle with olive oil and salt. Cook in a preheated oven at 200°C (400°F) Gas Mark 6 for 15 minutes. Meanwhile, drain the tuna, pat dry on kitchen paper, then brush with sesame oil.

Add the tuna to the roasting tin and continue to cook for about 10–15 minutes, until the fish is tender but still pink in the middle, and the potatoes are golden brown, and soft when pierced with a fork. A leafy green salad would be a suitable accompaniment.

500 g/1 lb tuna fillet

2 sweet potatoes, peeled and sliced into fat, chunky chips

olive oil, for roasting

sesame oil, for brushing

sea salt

orange and star anise marinade

50 ml/2 fl oz soy sauce

grated rind and juice of 2 oranges

2 tablespoons honey

1 tablespoon sesame oil

2 garlic cloves, crushed

2.5 cm/1 inch piece of fresh ginger, grated

2 strips lemon zest

1 star anise

1 tablespoon sesame seeds, toasted

Serves 4

Coriander squid
with seven-spice and mustard seeds

Japanese and Thai cooking both feature
seven-spice mixtures. This recipe uses Thai.

**2 tablespoons
rice vinegar**

**2 teaspoons
mustard seeds**

2 small chillies, sliced

1 egg white

2 tablespoons cream

16 small squid, cleaned

oil, for frying

spiced flour

125 g/4 oz plain flour

1½ teaspoons salt

**3 tablespoons
sesame seeds**

**2 teaspoons
mustard seeds**

**1 teaspoon
coriander seeds**

**1 teaspoon
seven-spice powder**

Serves 4

To make a chilli and mustard seed dipping sauce,
pour the rice vinegar into a small bowl, then add the
mustard seeds and sliced chillies. Set aside to infuse.
To prepare the squid, whip the egg white and cream
together, then dip the squid in the mixture.
Mix the spiced flour ingredients together, then press
the squid firmly into the mixture so the fish is well
covered with spices.
Heat the oil in a heavy-based pan, add the squid and
fry for about 3 minutes until golden brown.
Remove from the pan and drain on kitchen paper.
Serve with a bowl of the chilli dipping sauce.

Tamarind lamb chops
with guava jelly

Tamarind is used a little like lemon juice – to give a sharp flavour. You can buy it in brown velvety pods, in blocks of paste (illustrated below left), which you have to reconstitute in boiling water, or as a ready-made purée. It contrasts well with the rich sweetness of guava jelly, which you can buy in bottles in Caribbean or Asian markets – or even make your own using fresh or canned guava juice.

If using tamarind paste, crumble the paste, place it in a large saucepan, cover with water, bring to the boil and simmer over a medium-low heat for about 30 minutes, until soft. Push through a sieve, and discard the seeds and strings.
To make the sauce, heat the oil over a low heat, add the shallots, salt and pepper and sauté until golden. Add the garlic, cook for 2 minutes, then add the stock and tamarind pulp or purée. Bring to the boil, and simmer for 10 minutes. Stir in the cayenne and honey. Remove from the heat and keep warm.
Brush the lamb chops with oil. Mix the pepper, sesame and cumin seeds in a shallow bowl, then press the chops on to the mixture until they are well coated with seeds. Set aside.
Heat the oil in a heavy-based frying pan and fry the chops until the seeds are golden and the chops cooked to your liking. Serve with parsnip chips, the tamarind sauce and guava jelly.

8 lamb chops

freshly ground black pepper

3 tablespoons sesame seeds

3 tablespoons cumin seeds

oil, for brushing and frying

tamarind sauce

175 g/6 oz tamarind paste, or 125 g/4 oz tamarind purée

1 tablespoon olive oil

6 shallots, diced

2 garlic cloves, crushed

300 ml/½ pint chicken or vegetable stock

pinch of cayenne

1½ tablespoons honey

salt and freshly ground black pepper

to serve

parsnip chips

guava jelly

Serves 4

Malaysian lamb curry
with green curry paste

A sweet, mild curry made with galangal, a cousin of ginger, which is usually available either fresh or powdered in Asian markets. It is the same plant as the European galingale, which medieval monks used as a culinary and medicinal spice. This recipe uses powdered galangal, but 2 teaspoons of minced fresh galangal could be used instead. If you can't find galangal, half the quantity of ginger is a suitable substitute. Kaffir lime leaves can also be found in Asian markets, but if they're not available, you can substitute grated lime zest.

To make the green curry paste, peel the ginger and place in a blender with the chillies, garlic and fresh coriander, and purée until smooth. Set aside until ready to use.
To make the curry, heat the oil in a deep frying pan, add the shallot and sauté until soft. Add the cubes of lamb and fry until browned, then add the green curry paste, ginger, turmeric, coriander seeds, cinnamon, galangal, cumin seeds, lime leaves and coconut cream and gently simmer for 40 minutes.
Slice the aubergines, add to the pan and simmer for a further 20 minutes.
Serve sprinkled with the crispy fried onions. Fragrant Thai rice would be a suitable accompaniment.

150 ml/¼ pint olive oil

1 shallot, chopped

1 kg/2 lb leg of lamb,
boned and cubed

2 teaspoons
ground ginger

1 teaspoon turmeric

2 teaspoons coriander
seeds, roasted

1 cinnamon stick

1 teaspoon galangal

½ teaspoon
cumin seeds

3 kaffir lime leaves

600 ml/1 pint
coconut cream

2 small aubergines

crispy fried onions,
to serve

**green curry
paste**

50 g/2 oz fresh ginger

5 whole green chillies

4 garlic cloves

leaves of 1 bunch of
fresh coriander

Serves 4

Coconut chicken
with garlic and ginger sauce

Ginger is the spice used in this recipe. Once regarded as a spice only when dried, modern transport and farming methods mean that now we can have spices like this in their fresh form – a slightly different taste, but one which many people prefer.

2 tablespoons
unsalted butter

1 tablespoon olive oil

8 chicken pieces

2 shallots, chopped

1 garlic clove, crushed

2.5 cm/1 inch piece
of fresh ginger,
peeled and grated

250 ml/ 8 fl oz
coconut milk

2 tablespoons orange
or kumquat marmalade

salt and black
freshly ground pepper

50 g/2 oz shredded
coconut, toasted,
to serve

Serves 4

Heat the butter and olive oil in a large pan, add the chicken and cook for about 3–4 minutes until browned on all sides. Remove from the pan with a slotted spoon and set aside in a warm place. Add the shallots, garlic and ginger to the pan and sauté for 2 minutes, until softened and transparent. Return the chicken to the pan and stir in the coconut milk, marmalade and seasoning. Simmer, uncovered, for about 5 minutes until the chicken is tender. Scatter with the toasted coconut and serve. Fragrant Thai rice would be a suitable accompaniment.

Baked chicken breasts
with chillies and spicy cream

Indian cooks grind and fry their garam masalas (spice mixtures) before proceeding with the rest of a recipe – to release all the wonderful volatile oils. Each cook has her own masala mix, but a typical blend might include 2 tablespoons each of coriander and cardamom seeds, 1 teaspoon each of cumin, peppercorns and cloves, 1 cinnamon stick, and ½ teaspoon each of nutmeg and mace.

To make the spicy cream mixture, mix the tomato purée with the mustard, cumin, garam masala, lemon juice, salt, chilli powder and cream. Set aside. To prepare the chicken, cut the breasts off the bone. Crush the cardamom pods, and slice the ginger and deseeded chillies into strips. Heat 3 tablespoons of the oil in a pan, and sauté the cinnamon, cardamom and cloves for 1 minute. Add the chicken in a single layer, brown on both sides, then transfer to an oven-proof dish. Add the onion, ginger and chillies to the pan, stir-fry until golden, then spread over the chicken. Heat the remaining oil in the pan, add the mustard seeds, and fry until they pop. Add the garlic and cook until golden. Add the spicy cream and heat to a simmer. Pour over the chicken, season, and cook in a preheated oven at 180°C (350°F) Gas Mark 4 for 25 minutes, or until the chicken is done. Serve with the sauce poured over. Cabbage stir-fried with garlic and chilli flakes is a suitable accompaniment.

4 chicken breasts

6 cardamom pods

25 g/1 oz fresh ginger

3 hot green chillies

4 tablespoons corn oil

1 cinnamon stick

6 cloves

1 onion, sliced

½ teaspoon black or yellow mustard seeds

1 garlic clove, crushed

salt and pepper

spicy cream

2 tablespoons tomato purée

1 tablespoon Dijon mustard

pinch of ground cumin

pinch of garam masala

lemon juice, to taste

½ teaspoon salt

pinch of chilli powder

250 ml/ 8 fl oz cream

Serves 4

Indian cooks **fry their spices** to release

their **wonderful aromas** before adding them to a dish

Gingered chicken
with cinnamon prunes and almonds

A bouquet of spices including cinnamon, ginger and saffron make a sweet, golden dish with a Moroccan background.

To prepare the spicy vegetables, quarter the onions and core and quarter the peppers. Sprinkle with the cumin and coriander seeds, brush with oil and cook in a preheated oven at 200°C (400°F) Gas Mark 6 for about 30 minutes or until softened with crispy edges.

To prepare the chicken, rub the pieces with salt, pepper and ginger and set aside for 30 minutes. Meanwhile, place the prunes in a pan with cold water to cover. Add the cinnamon stick, bring to the boil and simmer for 20 minutes.

Melt the butter in a casserole and, when bubbling, add the almonds and fry until golden. Remove and drain on kitchen paper.

Add the sliced onions to the casserole and fry gently until softened and transparent. Add the saffron and ground cinnamon, sauté for 1 minute, then add the chicken and fry until golden.

Add the prunes with their poaching liquid, cover and simmer for 30 minutes. Remove the cinnamon stick.

Sprinkle the chicken with the almonds and serve with the spicy vegetables. Steamed couscous would be a suitable accompaniment.

8 chicken pieces

1 teaspoon ground ginger

250 g/8 oz pitted prunes

1 cinnamon stick

6 tablespoons butter

250 g/8 oz whole blanched almonds

2 Spanish onions, sliced

½ teaspoon saffron

2–3 teaspoons ground cinnamon

salt and freshly ground black pepper

spicy vegetables

4 small red onions

4 small red peppers

1 tablespoon cumin seeds

2 teaspoons coriander seeds

salt and freshly ground black pepper

oil, for brushing

Serves 4

Vegetables

Vegetable tagine
with shredded apricots

The tagine, named after the conical cooking pot used in North Africa, is one of the glories of Moroccan cooking, and can be made with lamb, chicken or vegetables. Substitute red lentils for the yellow split peas to produce a thick, spicy gravy to soak up the couscous.

Finely slice the pepper, cut the sweet potato into chunks, and skin, deseed and chop the tomatoes. Place the split peas in a pan, pour over the stock, add the garlic and onions, bring to the boil and simmer for 20 minutes. Stir in the remaining ingredients, bring to the boil and simmer for a further 15–20 minutes.
Scatter with the toasted cumin seeds and serve with steamed couscous.

1 green pepper

1 medium sweet potato

500 g/1 lb tomatoes

125 g/4 oz yellow split peas, rinsed

350 ml/12 fl oz vegetable stock

1 garlic clove, crushed

250 g/8 oz pickling onions or shallots

250 g/8 oz baby carrots

pinch of cinnamon

pinch of ground ginger

½ teaspoon cayenne

juice of 1 lemon

1 teaspoon honey

4 dried apricots, finely sliced

to serve

½ teaspoon toasted cumin seeds

couscous

Serves 4

Spicy potatoes
with garlic three-seed sauce

Potatoes form a wonderful base for spiced sauces. This recipe, served with rice and lentils, is great for vegetarians and it's a treat for non-vegetarians too, when served with plain or spicy meat dishes.

Heat half the oil in a large, heavy-based frying pan, add the sliced potatoes and gently sauté until cooked and golden brown. Drain on kitchen paper. To make the sauce, add the remaining oil to the pan, stir in the spices, bay leaves, chillies and garlic, and cook for 1 minute. Mix in the onion, gently fry until golden, then add the sugar and chopped tomatoes. Bring the mixture to the boil, reduce the heat, then simmer for a further 10 minutes. Add 600 ml/1 pint water, return to the boil, then simmer, stirring regularly, for 10 minutes.
Add the golden potatoes and mix gently until evenly coated with the spicy sauce.
Simmer for 5 minutes, then serve.

125 ml/4 fl oz olive oil

1 kg/2 lb potatoes, thinly sliced, rinsed and dried

three-seed sauce

1 teaspoon fenugreek seeds

1½ tablespoons fennel seeds

1 tablespoons black mustard seeds

1½ teaspoons turmeric

3 fresh bay leaves

4 hot chillies, finely sliced

1–6 garlic cloves, crushed (depending on taste)

3 large onions, finely chopped

1 teaspoon sugar

1 kg/2 lb ripe tomatoes, skinned, deseeded and chopped

Serves 4

42 Vegetables

Braised aubergine
with spiced yoghurt

This is a modern update of the great
Turkish classic dish *Imam bayaldi,* which
means 'the priest fainted'. No one has ever
worked out why he fainted – though it was
presumably from pleasure at being offered
such a delicious concoction.

Cut the aubergines into 1 cm/½ inch slices.
Skin, deseed and dice the tomatoes.
Heat half the oil in a frying pan and cook the onion
gently until softened and golden.
Add the tomatoes, garlic, cloves, cayenne, cinnamon,
cumin seeds, currants and mint, and cook over a low
heat for 10 minutes.
Heat the remaining oil in another pan until very hot,
add the aubergine and fry until deep brown.
Mix the aubergine into the onion and tomato mixture.
Allow to cool, then season to taste.
To make the spiced yoghurt, mix the yoghurt, cumin
seeds and coriander and coriander leaves together
in a small bowl and serve with the aubergines.
This dish may be served by itself, as a vegetable
accompaniment for a meat dish such as lamb, or as
part of a traditional Indian meal, with basmati rice,
chutneys and other spiced dishes.

anoth

this o

3 medium aubergines

6 large plum tomatoes

75 ml/3 fl oz olive oil

1 onion, finely diced

1 garlic clove, crushed

1 teaspoon cloves

pinch of cayenne

2 cinnamon sticks

1 teaspoon cumin seeds

3 tablespoons currants

2 tablespoons chopped
fresh mint leaves

salt and pepper

spiced yoghurt

150 ml/¼ pint yoghurt

1 tablespoon toasted
cumin seeds

½ teaspoon ground
coriander

2 tablespoons chopped
fresh coriander leaves

Serves 4

...odern update on a **culinary classic** –

...om **Turkish** cookery

Oven-roasted peppers
stuffed with spiced risotto

If you're serving this dish to vegetarians, use vegetable stock instead of chicken stock. Risotto rice makes a much more creamy, delicious stuffing than if you used ordinary long-grain rice, and the pine nuts produce a delicious, buttery crunch in contrast.

Cut the peppers in half and deseed. Heat the oil in a large pan, add the onions and salt and sauté until golden, stirring occasionally. Add the pine nuts and sauté until golden. Stir in the rice and cook for 3 minutes. Add a little hot stock, followed by the currants, tomato purée, sugar, allspice, chilli powder, oregano, cumin and cinnamon. Cook over a low heat until the rice is half cooked, then cool. Stir in the mint and lemon juice, tossing well. Stuff the pepper halves with the filling, place in a roasting tin and cook in a preheated oven at 180°C (350°F) Gas Mark 4 for 30 minutes. Serve with lemon wedges.

10 small red peppers

3 tablespoons olive oil

2 onions, grated

1½ teaspoons salt

50 g/2 oz pine nuts

125 g/4 oz risotto rice

450 ml/¾ pint hot chicken stock

3 tablespoons dried currants

1 tablespoon tomato purée

1 teaspoon sugar

1 teaspoon ground allspice

pinch of chilli powder

pinch of oregano

pinch of cumin

pinch of cinnamon

2 tablespoons finely sliced fresh mint leaves

2 tablespoons lemon juice

8 lemon wedges, to serve

Serves 4

Cabbage potato gratin
with ham and juniper berries

Juniper berries are a very European spice –
particularly popular because they didn't
have to be imported from the exotic orient,
but could be gathered in the hedgerows.
They are the major flavouring ingredient of
gin, and are well suited to dishes of pork,
charcuterie or game – and cabbage too.

Melt the butter in a heavy-based pan, add the onion
and juniper berries and sauté gently until softened
and transparent. Stir in the cabbage, cover with a lid
and gently cook for about 10 minutes until just
wilted. Stir in the ham, cream and apple juice and
spoon into a large oval gratin dish.
Place the potato on top, with the slices overlapping,
then sprinkle with cheese and bake in a preheated
oven at 180°C (350°F) Gas Mark 4 until the potatoes
are tender. Serve alone as a winter luncheon dish, or
as an accompaniment for meat dishes, especially
pork and game.

50 g/2 oz butter

1 onion, sliced

1 tablespoon juniper
berries, crushed

1 Savoy cabbage,
shredded

125 g/4 oz serrano ham,
shredded

300 ml/½ pint
single cream

250 ml/8 fl oz
apple juice

500 g/1 lb potatoes,
sliced

50 g/2 oz Gruyère
cheese, grated

Serves 4

that ver

is a perfect partner fc

ropean spice, the **juniper berry**,

rk, ham, game and cabbage

Pickles

Above, from left, Pickled lemons
(recipe page 52), Candied kumquats
(page 53) and Pumpkin spice pickle
(page 52).

Pickled lemons

Use the peel only – with poached meats,
couscous dishes or in salads.

Cut the lemons in quarters with a sharp knife,
leaving them attached at the stem end for the last
1 cm/½ inch. Place 1–2 tablespoons of salt in each
preserving jar. Stuff the lemons with the remaining
salt and re-form them into their original shape. Pack
them tightly into the jars, adding the bay leaves and
spices as you pack. Add any remaining salt, then
pour in lemon juice to cover.
Seal and store for 4–5 weeks before using.

12 lemons

250 g/8 oz salt,
or more if necessary

2–3 fresh bay leaves

2 cinnamon sticks

2 cloves

16 peppercorns

juice of 3–4 lemons

Makes 2 jars of
600 ml/1 pint

Pumpkin spice pickle

Pumpkin pickle is such a glorious colour –
the bonus is that it also tastes fabulous, and
gives a real lift to cheese and meats.

Peel, deseed and dice the pumpkin. Place the sugar
and vinegar in a pan and boil until syrupy. Pour over
the pumpkin and leave overnight. Next day, drain off
the liquid into a preserving pan. Add the remaining
ingredients, bring to the boil then add the pumpkin.
Simmer for 3 hours or until the mixture is thick.
Pack the pickle into warm, sterilized Kilner jars.
Seal while still hot. Keep for 1 month before using.

2 kg/4 lb pumpkin

1.5 kg/3 lb sugar

1.8 litres/3 pints
white wine vinegar

1 tablespoon celery salt

15 cm/6 inch piece of
fresh ginger, grated

2 cinnamon sticks

1 tablespoon white
mustard seeds

10 cloves

Makes 4 jars of
600 ml/1 pint

Candied kumquats

A colourful, unusual recipe to use as an accompaniment to ice-cream and other puddings. An alternative recipe is to fill a Kilner jar with kumquats, add 2 tablespoons of sugar, a few cloves and a cinnamon stick to each jar, then cover with brandy. Seal and set aside for 2–6 months. Use the sliced fruit with char-grilled duck breasts and the kumquat brandy to flame the meat, or as a liqueur with puddings or coffee.

500 g/1 lb kumquats

500 g/1 lb granulated sugar

250 ml/8 fl oz cider vinegar

125 ml/4 fl oz water

2 cinnamon sticks

10 whole cloves

2 whole star anise

Makes 3 jars of 600 ml/1 pint

Wash the kumquats well, discarding any stems. Place in a pan, cover with water and bring to the boil. Reduce the heat and simmer for about 5 minutes. Drain in a colander and refresh under cold water. Place all the remaining ingredients in a large saucepan and bring to the boil. Add the kumquats. Reduce the heat to low and poach gently for about 15 minutes until the fruits are very tender. Sterilize 2 Kilner jars by placing in a deep saucepan, pouring over boiling water to cover, then simmering gently for 15 minutes. Using a slotted spoon, transfer the kumquats to the sterilized Kilner jars. Cool the syrup to room temperature and pour over the kumquats. Seal the jars and keep in the refrigerator for up to 2 months.

Sweet things

Steamed puddings
with chocolate and spicy figs

A favourite recipe based on a feature in
Marie-Claire magazine on that most sensual
of ingredients – chocolate. These are rather
homely puddings but very warming and
perfect with maple syrup and vanilla custard
or the gingered crème fraîche on page 59.

Cream the butter and sugar together until light and
fluffy, then gradually beat in the eggs. Sift the dry
ingredients together, then fold into the egg mixture.
Spoon the mixture into 4 lightly buttered teacups or
small pudding basins. Cover each cup with a piece
of greaseproof paper, place in a pan of boiling water,
cover and steam for about 1 hour.
Serve with warm maple syrup poured over, and
vanilla custard (if using).

125 g/4 oz unsalted
butter, softened

125 g/4 oz soft dark
brown sugar

2 eggs

75 g/3 oz plain flour,
sieved

2 tablespoon cocoa

pinch of
ground cinnamon

pinch of ground ginger

pinch of
ground coriander

75 g/3 oz chopped
dried figs

to serve

warm maple syrup

vanilla custard
(optional)

Serves 4

Vanilla pod custard
with spicy biscuits

An easy, pretty pudding to serve mid-week,
when friends come around for dinner and
expect something fabulous to end the meal.

To make the biscuits, sift the dry ingredients together. Gently warm the syrup until hot and runny. Stir in the butter and, when melted, scrape into a bowl. Mix in the dry ingredients to form a dough. Chill for 1 hour, then roll out to 5 mm/¼ inch thick. Cut out rounds with a biscuit cutter and place on a lightly buttered baking sheet. Cook in a preheated oven at 190°C (375°F) Gas Mark 5 for 10–12 minutes. Remove from the oven and cool on a wire rack. To make the vanilla pod custard, heat the cream and vanilla pods in a saucepan. Remove the pods, split them, scrape the seeds into the cream, then return the pods to the pan. Remove the pan from the heat and infuse for 10 minutes. Remove the pods. Beat the egg yolks and whole egg together, add the sugar and beat until pale and creamy. Stir in the cornflour, then whisk in the infused cream. Spoon the mixture into 6 ramekin dishes or glasses, cover with foil or greaseproof paper and place in a roasting tin half filled with water. Cook in a preheated oven at 150°C (325°F) Gas Mark 3 for 45–60 minutes until just set and firm to the touch. Serve with the spicy biscuits, a sweet pudding wine, and the segmented oranges, if using.

250 ml/8 fl oz
single cream

1–2 vanilla pods

3 egg yolks

1 whole egg

125 g/4 oz caster sugar

1 teaspoon cornflour

segmented oranges,
to serve (optional)

spicy biscuits

125 g/4 oz
self-raising flour

½ teaspoon
bicarbonate of soda

1 teaspoon ground
mixed spice

25 g/1 oz caster sugar

75 g/3 oz golden syrup

50 g/2 oz
unsalted butter

Serves 4

an easy but **spectacular** pudding –

spicy biscuits with a **fragrant** vanilla custard

Orange cardamom tart
with ginger cream

A spectacular pudding – just don't tell anyone it's so easy to make. For a stronger flavour of orange and cardamom, don't strain the mixture before baking. You could use the more traditional powdered ginger to make the cream, but I much prefer the zingy bright taste of fresh ginger.

To make the pastry, rub the butter into the flour until it resembles fine breadcrumbs. Fold in the egg yolks and sugar, adding enough cold water to bind. Chill for 10 minutes, then roll out on a floured surface. Use to line a 23 cm/9-inch loose-based flan tin. Chill for 20 minutes, then prick the base with a fork and bake blind in a preheated oven at 200°F (400°F) Gas Mark 6, for about 15 minutes until just golden. Place the cardamom seeds in a saucepan with the grated orange zest and juice, heat gently, then remove from the heat and leave to infuse. Mix the cornflour with a little water, then stir into the infused orange juice, together with the eggs, egg yolk and sugar. Pour into a heavy-based saucepan and cook gently, at just below simmering point, until thickened. Remove from the heat and whisk in the butter. Allow to cool slightly. Pour into the tart shell and bake in the oven at 200°F (400°F) Gas Mark 6 for 18–20 minutes until set. Leave to cool. Beat the ginger cream ingredients together and serve with the cooled tart.

125 g/4 oz
unsalted butter

250 g/8 oz plain flour

2 egg yolks

1 tablespoon sugar

**orange and
cardamom filling**

1 tablespoon
cardamom seeds

250 ml/8 fl oz orange
juice, plus grated rind
of 2 oranges

1 tablespoon cornflour

3 eggs

1 egg yolk

125 g/4 oz sugar

125 g/4 oz unsalted
butter, roughly diced

ginger cream

200 ml/7 fl oz
crème fraîche

1 cm/½ inch piece of
fresh ginger, grated

Serves 4

Spicy pear pastries
sprinkled with cinnamon

These individual pastries make perfect puddings or coffee-time nibbles. You can vary the fruit according to the season – pretty for springtime is a row of pink early forced rhubarb. Use ready-rolled puff pastry if you can – it saves lots of time!

4 small pears, peeled, halved and cored

4 star anise, crushed

4 cloves, crushed

1 vanilla pod

zest of 1 lemon, cut into fine julienne

2 tablespoons unrefined caster sugar

375 g/12 oz ready-rolled puff pastry

1 egg, beaten

2 tablespoons unrefined demerara sugar

pinch of ground cinnamon

mascarpone cheese or whipped cream, to serve

Makes 8 pastries

To poach the pears, place the spices, lemon zest and sugar in a saucepan with about 300 ml/½ pint water and bring to the boil. Add the pears and simmer lightly for about 10–15 minutes until just tender. Leave to cool in the liquid so they absorb the flavours of the spices.

Meanwhile, roll out the pastry on a floured surface to a rectangle 20 x 45 cm/12 x 18 inches, then cut into eight 10 cm/4 inch squares.

Place on a baking tray sprinkled with cold water. Trim a strip off each side 5 mm/¼ inch wide, brush with beaten egg and lay on top of each side of the squares to form a frame. Prick the base of the pastry with a fork then chill for 30–60 minutes.

Lift the pears from the poaching liquid, drain well on kitchen paper, place one half on each pastry shell, then sprinkle with sugar and cinnamon.

Bake in a preheated oven at 200°C (400°F) Gas Mark 6 for 10–15 minutes until the pastry is well risen and golden. Serve warm with mascarpone cheese or whipped cream.

Chocolate muffins
with orange and allspice

Beautiful for breakfast, luscious for lunch and absolutely fabulous with tea or coffee – these muffins are made with allspice, which really does taste of a melange of spices.

250 g/8 oz plain flour

1 tablespoon baking powder

½ teaspoon bicarbonate of soda

2 tablespoons cocoa powder

75 g/3 oz soft brown sugar

½ teaspoon ground allspice

50 g/2 oz plain dark chocolate

grated rind of 1 orange

1 egg

250 ml/8 fl oz milk

Makes 9

Place the flour, baking powder, bicarbonate of soda, cocoa powder, brown sugar and allspice in a bowl. Break the chocolate into pieces and stir it into the bowl together with the orange rind.

Beat the egg and milk together until well blended (do not over mix), then fold into the dry ingredients. Place 9 paper muffin cases in a bun tray, and spoon in the mixture.

Bake in a preheated oven at 200°C (400°F) Gas Mark 6 for 15 minutes, or until risen and firm to the touch.

Index